In The Shadow of His Cross

The Cliff Jacobs Story

Told To:

Dana Maria Hill

ISBN: 1-4140-8160-X (e-book)
ISBN: 1-4140-8159-6 (Paperback)
ISBN: 1-4140-8158-8 (Dust Jacket)

Library of Congress Control Number: 2004091655

Printed in the United States of America
Bloomington, IN

This book is printed on acid free paper.

1st Books - rev. 04/08/04

To all the angels in my life.

Sarah: my angel of love, my angel of hope.

Spencer: my angel of youthfulness, my brother.

Mom & Dad: my angels of unconditional love and much sacrifice.

Kelly & Mark: my angels of gentleness and kindness, my caregivers.

Jessica: my angel of music, a song in my heart.

Aunt Stella: my angel of determination. I graduated because you gently pushed me.

Uncle Jerry: a gentle spirit who taught me how to give.

Grandparents, aunts, uncles, and cousins: my angels of family and support.

Brother Ed Cash: my mentor. (Thanks for being a prime example of what a man of God should be.)

Brother Deon Black and the church at Belcher's Gap: my angels of encouragement and help in the ministry.

Brother Gary Williams and the wonderful people at Cornerstone Church for believing in me and promoting my book.

All my young preacher brethren who held me up on wings of faith.

The family of God: my angels of prayer who lifted me when I could not lift myself.

Doctor Raymond Gordon Watts: my doctor, my friend, my angel in the time of need.

All the staff at Children's Hospital for your patience and care.

The Sunshine Kids, G.W., Admiral Steve, Jennifer, for making my dreams come true.

The teachers and staff at Sardis High School: my angels of support.

The Sardis High School Graduating Class of 2003: my angels of laughter, sharing, and caring.(You guys were the best!)

My Lord, My Savior Jesus Christ: my promise of a better day.

There is a song and the chorus says, "I believe there are angels among us, sent down to us, from somewhere up above. They come to you and me in our darkest hours, to show us how to live, to teach us how to give, to shine us with a light of love."

You were all earthly angels, vessels that God used to help and encourage me. Maybe you sent a card, said a prayer, made a phone call, gave a love offering, whatever you did it was greatly appreciated. Maybe you were a silent prayer warrior who never got noticed, the God of Heaven took notice, thank you.

God Bless you, all my angels.

Acknowledgements

Special thanks to the following people who helped with the scrapbook photos and dedication page:

Kathy Fleck

Photography by Rickey Whitehead

John Chumley Photography

Bill Miller Photographers

The Sand Mountain Reporter

West End High School

Boaz Middle School

Sardis High School

Carnival Cruise Lines

Dedication

This book is dedicated to the memory of Sonya Terrell, Lacie Lockridge, and Jacob Garrett. They were young, beautiful, and full of life. Leukemia claimed their lives at a very young age. I was privileged to spend time with each of them.

I believe that God prepares His children for the journey that lies ahead of them. I remember when Sonya died at the age of sixteen; I was thirteen at the time. As I made my way up to the casket and looked at her angel face, the spirit of God spoke to my heart and began preparing me for a journey much like Sonya's.

Lacie and Jacob walked into my life at Children's Hospital in Birmingham, Alabama. They were in my life for a very short time. We would share our stories, our fears, and even our friends. We would cry together and we would laugh together. They touched my life and I will remember them always. Their smiles will forever be etched in my memory.

To all those who went before me and to all those who will come after me.............

Sonya Terrell

August 24, 1981-January 18, 1998

Jacob Garret

March 23, 1988-January 19, 2002

Lacie Lockridge

September 13, 1983-January 7, 2002

Foreword

"Before I formed thee in the belly I knew thee; and before thou camest forth out of the womb I sanctified thee, and I ordained thee a prophet unto the nations." Then said I, "Ah Lord God! Behold, I cannot speak; for I am a child." But the Lord said unto me, "Say not, I am a child; for thou shalt go to all that I shall send thee, and whatsoever I command thee thou shalt speak. Be not afraid of their faces; for I am with thee to deliver thee, saith the Lord." Then the Lord put forth His hand, and touched my mouth. And the Lord said unto me, "Behold I have put my words in thy mouth" (Jeremiah 1:5-9 KJV).

When my parents married and began planning for a family, they never imagined that the doctor would look at them and tell them there was no way they could have children. I am sure they were devastated; but, much to their surprise, only ten months after being told this, I, Clifford William Jacobs, was born into the world on the 11th day of April, 1985. That was only the beginning of the miracles in our life.

The Bible tells of many wonderful miracles that Jesus performed while He journeyed here on Earth. I am confident in saying that there are not enough books in the world to hold all the miracles that He has performed since He ascended to Heaven. I was taught all my life about the miracles of Jesus, healing the sick, causing the blind to see, the lame to walk, and even raising people from the dead, but I had no idea of the many miracles He was about to reveal unto me.

My journey with God has been unbelievable and incredible, to say the least. If God would help me I would like to share my story with you in a way that would bring glory and honor to my Lord. My prayer is that, by sharing my testimony with you, you will be encouraged on your journey, wherever it may lead you. The journey of life can leave you feeling helpless, low in spirit, and discouraged at times. Just look up; there is a God in Heaven and He is bigger than any problem you have.

I am a walking, talking testimony of what the Lord can do. You can overcome, you can endure, even when the storms of life are raging.

Author's Introduction

It was in the spring of 1997 that I first met Cliff Jacobs. Cliff and my son Bobby were on the same baseball team. Cliff was 12 years old and full of life. He never met a stranger and he had a smile that reached from ear to ear. I spent a lot of time with Cliff and his family that year at the baseball field. Cliff's mom and I quickly bonded and shared many long talks about our children, our hopes, our fears, and our dreams for their futures. There was something special about Cliff. He came to my house many times and he quickly became one of the family. Cliff could feel at home anywhere. He was a very loving and giving child and everyone loved him.

I remember so well the evening that I got the phone call telling me that Cliff had announced his call into the ministry. I was not surprised; I was pleased. Cliff was completely dedicated to God and the ministry. Whatever Cliff Jacobs set out to do he did it with his whole heart. He began preaching at the tender age of twelve.

In the spring of 2000, before his fifteenth birthday, the news came that Cliff had been diagnosed with cancer. It was in the form of a lump in his mouth and the biopsy showed it to be a rare adolescent cancer called rhabdomyosarcoma. I remember the tears, the fear and anxiety that built up in us all that day, but most of all I remember the courage this young man showed as he began a long, hard battle with cancer and a journey with God to places unknown.

Cliff's heart's desire is that his story will help just one person, one family in the battle. Cliff wants the world to know that there is a God in Heaven who loves and cares about you and all you are going through.

The purpose of this book is to reach out to a lost, suffering, hurting, discouraged generation and reassure them that there is hope in the Lord Jesus. This book tells the story of a young man and his battle with cancer. Cliff Jacobs is living proof that faith in God can move mountains. Cliff has battled cancer, gone through surgery, chemo, radiation, his parent's divorce, and even thoughts of suicide. He has held on to the nail-scarred hand of Jesus and he has overcome because he knows that all things are possible with God.

Whatever you are going through, whatever storm is raging out of control in your life, Cliff Jacobs wants to encourage you to not give up; you do not have to live a defeated life. You may be struggling mentally, physically, or even spiritually, but you can be happy in Jesus. As long as there is life, there is hope.

This is the testimony of Cliff Jacobs, the bravest young soldier I have ever known.

Dana Maria Hill

Table Of Contents

Chapter 1
Dreams & Disappointments 1

Chapter 2
"Be Still And Know That I Am God." (Psalms 46:10 KJV) 10

Chapter 3
The Tropical Storm 18

Chapter 4
Happy Birthday To Me 25

Chapter 5
Attitude & Endurance 29

Chapter 6
Test of Faith 32

Chapter 7
Things Are Not Always What They Seem 40

Chapter 8
The Class of 2003 64

Chapter 9
Thoughts of Suicide 68

Chapter 10
A Mother's Heart 73

Chapter 11
A Father's Determination 79

Chapter 12
My Brother, My Friend 83

Chapter 13
Fear Not 87

Chapter 14
Sarah, The Love of my Life 92

Chapter 15
Bear Your Cross.. 97

Chapter 1

Dreams & Disappointments

My entire life I had dreamed of being a professional baseball player. When I was only four years old I began playing tee-ball and quickly became addicted to the sport. Mom and Dad always encouraged this dream. Later on I attended many baseball camps and was improving every year. I worked hard every day and I knew in my heart that if I practiced and put my whole heart into it that someday it would pay off. By the time I was fifteen I had scouts watching me and I was confident that my dream was going to become a reality.

When I was eight years old I gave my life to Jesus at New Union F.C.M. Church, and at the tender age of twelve I announced my call into the ministry of God. I surrendered my heart, soul, body, and mind to the cause of Christ. Even at a young age I was criticized for being a "holy roller." However, that is a title I have grown to be proud of. "Jesus Christ himself being the chief cornerstone." That is my primary objective in life – Christ being my chief cornerstone. Little did I know the road ahead of me would try, tempt, and test the endurance of my faith.

My dad was an ordained minister and the pastor of a small church in the community where we lived, and my Mom taught Sunday school, played the piano and sang. My younger brother, Spencer, and I, lived in a very loving home and God just continued to bless us. The church was growing and souls were being won to Christ. My family was respected in our community and we had a wonderful church family who loved us. As much as I loved baseball, I loved God more. My work for Him always came first and then baseball.

Learning came easy for me, and I excelled in academics. I was an honor roll student and was determined to get an athletic or academic scholarship. My circle of friends was growing and I had a beautiful, sweet girlfriend. Life was good, and I was happy. God had blessed me. My life was a rainbow of beautiful colors, but little did I know there was a storm brewing.

In the spring of 2000 I found a lump in my throat and, after a routine checkup from the family doctor, was given antibiotics and told it was infection – probably from sinus drainage. Days passed; more antibiotics. The lump remained and I was referred to an ear, nose and throat doctor. He removed the lump and sent it off for a biopsy. It was cancer. Rhabdomyosarcoma is a rare, dangerous, fast-growing form of cancer. The tumors arise from a primitive muscle cell and then grow out of control. The tumors can appear in numerous locations, including the head, neck, genito-urinary tract, extremities, chest and lungs. The tumors are so rare that only a few hundred cases per year are diagnosed in the United States. Most victims are children ages 2-6 and 15-19. Most patients do not survive the first case. I was given a 20% chance of surviving.

Those were some tough facts to swallow for a fifteen-year-old with big dreams and high expectations. The only thing most fifteen-year-old boys have on their mind is getting a driver's permit, making the all-star baseball team, and girls. My anxiety and fear had become a reality. I remember sitting at Children's Hospital in Birmingham and talking to Dr. Raymond Gordon Watts. He had a gentle spirit and his bedside manner let me know that he cared about me and that I could trust him. It was very reassuring to discover that he believed in God and had faith in the higher power. For the next three years we would be seeing a lot of each other and we would become friends.

It was revival time at the church where my dad was serving as pastor. We got the news on Monday that I had cancer. On Thursday night of that revival my dad asked if anyone had anything they would like to do or anything they would like to share with the congregation. A young lady, probably in her teens, stood up and asked if she could sing a song. As she began to sing the spirit of God spoke to my heart. The song was about a little bird who came to someone during a storm and sang a song to let them know everything was going to be all right. Nobody had ever met or seen this young lady and she got away before my dad could speak to her. I knew in my heart that God had sent her to encourage me and my family through the words in the song. I believe that God prepares His children for whatever tomorrow may bring about in our lives and He sends hope. That night He sent hope to me and my family through the words of that song. He sent a young angel out of nowhere to sing to my soul. God is so good!

The next morning I had to be at Children's Hospital in Birmingham for scans. My dad and grandmother went with me. We had about an hour to spare in between scans so we decided to get out of the hospital and go for a walk. You can imagine all the noise of downtown Birmingham in the middle of the day. There were construction workers, sirens, traffic, people talking, and horns blowing. As we walked down the street, my grandmother began to have leg cramps. (Though she was in pain, God was working through her.) We stopped walking and we were standing under this power pole and suddenly, out of Heaven, came this little bird. It was perched on this power pole singing the sweetest song as loud as it could sing. All the noise had

4

stopped and all I could hear was this beautiful song. I remember looking at my dad and, with tears in our eyes and joy in our hearts, we just smiled and stood there amazed that God had sent some blessed assurance to let us know that everything was going to be all right. I remembered the scripture in God's word, Matthew 6:26 KJV: "Behold the fowls of the air: for they sow not, neither do they reap, nor gather into barns; yet your Heavenly Father feedeth them. Are you not much better than they?" I knew that whatever tomorrow held for me and my family that God would be there to take care of us and to provide us with whatever we needed.

My picture-perfect life was not perfect anymore. All the beautiful colors were fading away and there was darkness instead of a rainbow. The storm clouds were gathering all around me on every side. It attacked me as an angry foe and it took me prisoner against my will. It tossed me to and fro and overwhelmed me. The storm was raging out of control. I was scared, sad, shocked, and so many anxieties and fears were rising up in my head. I could run or scream, but it would not take the cancer away. I found my quiet time with God and I remembered His words in the book of John 14:18 KJV: "I will not leave you comfortless: I will come to you." There is story about Jesus and His disciples in the book of Mark 4:35-41 KJV. Jesus told His disciples to pass over to the other side. They were in a ship and a great storm of wind came and the waves beat the ship. Jesus was asleep in the hind part of the ship. The disciples were so afraid and they awoke Him and asked

5

Him, "Master, carest thou not that we perish?" So Jesus arose and rebuked the wind and said unto the sea, "Peace, be still." And the wind ceased, and there was a great calm. Then Jesus asked them, "Why are ye so fearful? How is it that ye have no faith?" I believe we are all given a measure of faith and we must exercise that faith for it to increase and become stronger. I was about to learn a lot about storms and faith.

Lots of people ask me if I was angry at God when I found out I had cancer. Sure I was, for a moment. I could not believe it was happening to me. I had always been a faithful follower, a minister of the gospel, and I had given Him my life! Why would He allow me to suffer this? We are so quick to blame God for every bad thing that happens and I am sure, for a while, I blamed Him. I realize now that the day I was diagnosed with cancer was the beginning of my wisdom and understanding as a child of God and as a minister. Let me assure you that bad things happen to good people. I remembered Job, a faithful man of God, and I remembered all that Job had to go through and all that he lost. This was my bitter cup to drink and my heavy cross to carry. Little did I know that God's plan for my life was much bigger than I ever expected. The door of opportunity was opening up and I felt like Jabez when God expanded His territory. I Chronicles 4:10 KJV: "And Jabez called on the God of Israel, saying, 'Oh that thou wouldest bless me indeed, and enlarge my coast, and that thine hand might be with me, and that thou wouldest keep me from evil, that it may not grieve me!'" And God granted him that which he requested. I had always prayed for God to bless my work in the ministry and for my life to be a testimony to others, but I had no idea how God was about to use my life to touch others, and so my journey began as I sat helplessly in the shadow of His cross and wept.

When I was first diagnosed with cancer I could feel people looking at me and asking themselves, "I wonder what he did to deserve this? Was it his sin or his parents? Is this God's punishment or His wrath?" I remember thinking, "For He maketh His sun to rise on the evil and on the good, and sendeth rain on the just and on the unjust" (Matthew 5:45 KJV). I recall a story in the word of God about a blind man who had been blind since birth. The Lord's disciples asked Him who had sinned that this had happened to the child. Jesus answered and said, "Neither hath this man sinned, nor his parents, but that the works of God should be made manifest in Him." Then the Lord spat on the ground, and made clay of the spittle, and He anointed the eyes of the blind man with clay and He could see. The Lord received glory and honor for the miracle and He will receive glory and honor from me. Cancer doesn't care who you are, who your parents are, how much money you have, how big your house is, or how much faith you have. Cancer is no respecter of person, and neither is death. Young and old will surely die. It may not be cancer that brings you death but it will be something. The Lord has set before us life and death, blessings and cursing, therefore choose life which is in Christ Jesus. I am so thankful that God sent His son Jesus to die for our sins that we might have eternal life. One day I will leave this land of sin and I will enter into an eternal life because I made a choice when I was very young to serve God and I accepted His son Jesus as my savior. In Romans 6:23 the scripture says, "for the wages of sin is death; but the gift of God is eternal life through Jesus Christ our Lord."

Is there a storm in your life? Has your perfect world suddenly become not so perfect? Sometimes things happen that we have no control over, but there is a God in Heaven who has control over every situation. Life sometimes throws us curveballs, and dreams don't always come true, but we do not have to live defeated lives. There is joy and happiness in serving God. Sometimes our plans for the future are not God's plans for our future. When He leads us in a different direction we should follow Him willingly because He knows what is best for our lives. Remember this and meditate on it, "Being confident of this very thing, that he which hath begun a good work in you will perform it until the day of Jesus Christ" (Philippians 1:6 KJV). You can be happy in Jesus no matter what comes your way. Weather the storm with Jesus and He will speak peace to your soul.

I received this during a raging storm in my life. May you find peace in its words as I did.

Overcoming The Storm

I awoke from a sweet sleep to see storm clouds gathering all around me on every side. The wind was blowing violently out of control. I was frightened as the storm raged and ranted. It attacked and assaulted as an angry foe. It took me prisoner against my will and robbed my sweet sleep and took away my security blanket. It tossed me to and fro. It overwhelmed my soul. The tempest raged.

I sought for shelter and fled to the arms of Jesus. He surrounded me with a hedge to protect me from the hostile force. The storm fortified me and I then was made stronger than before. Jesus gave me the strength to resist the evil and I endured with His arms protecting me as a mother protects her child. The shadow of His cross was my hope. His unconditional love was my strength. Like an eagle we flew above the storm, strong and safe from all harm. The storm began to weaken and its wind became as a gentle breeze. The dark storm clouds turned into rainbows and my fear was replaced with peace. Once again, I laid down and found sweet rest.

"Those that wait upon the Lord shall renew their strength; they shall mount up with wings as eagles; they shall run and not be weary; and they shall walk and not faint" (Isaiah 40:31 KJV).

Chapter 2

"Be Still And Know That I Am God." (Psalms 46:10 KJV)

In the spring of 2000, after being diagnosed with cancer, I began five months of chemo treatments. Chemo makes you sick to your stomach and you throw up a lot. It drains your energy and leaves you weak. Not to mention it causes your hair to fall out. I went through five months of chemo. Chemotherapy is a treatment used to destroy cancer cells. It is used to control the cancer and relieve the symptoms. I knew that my life depended on these treatments but I was not happy about taking them. You have to lay there while the drugs are flowing through your body and your mind is coming and going. Finally you fall asleep, wake up, throw up, and go back to sleep. I hated it. I dreaded it.

Finally the five months of chemo came to an end and then I began the dreadful radiation treatments.

Chemo was a breeze compared to radiation. The radiation burnt the inside of my mouth and caused dryness and irritation. It destroyed my salivary glands; I had no saliva and my taste buds were gone. Everything tasted like ashes and I lost my appetite. It got really bad and I could not eat or drink. When I finally was able to eat, my pancreas rejected the food and I got very sick with a bout of pancreatitis. The doctors gave me about a 20% chance of survival and they also said I should consider giving up preaching because I could lose my voice. I knew that this was going to be a serious obstacle; however, I also knew that God had called me so it was His decision when I would stop preaching. I needed a touch from the Master Physician.

I was on some strong drugs and my parents were told that if I survived I would be addicted to the drugs for the rest of my life. I was so tired and my strength was gone; it would have been easy to give up the fight, but God kept the fight in me. My friends and family tried to keep me encouraged but nothing was making me happy. I knew that after radiation I was looking at six more months of chemo. I remember thinking that it would be easier to die. There were many discouraging days and nights at Children's Hospital. I found myself wanting to give up. I even prayed for God to take me out of the misery, even if it meant death. When I was on a pity party God would always send an angel to encourage me. Sometimes it would be a phone call, a visit, or a little card in the mail. God sent many angels to encourage me. They came in all shapes and sizes and all ages. Some were family members, others were my church family, and some were classmates, but all made a difference in my life. The staff at Children's Hospital was so loving and caring during those days and nights. Everyone would try to lift my spirits.

It was Halloween and Children's Hospital (my home away from home) was having a contest for the best costume. My dad got this bright idea that he would dress up like a wrestler and would get me out of bed, put me into a wheelchair and we would go downstairs to this costume contest that was taking place. I will never forget that sight as long as I live. He came out of the bathroom wearing cut-off shorts and a t-shirt and his bald head was just a shining! When my hair started falling out from the chemo, my dad and my brother went with me and we all got our heads shaved. That was a sacrifice on their part and I was very touched by it. That was the funniest-looking man I had ever seen and I laughed and he laughed for the first time in a long time. I thought if he can make this sacrifice just to get me out of bed and lift my spirits, then surely I could take a ride in the wheelchair.

Dad was pushing me down the hall and we got to the elevator, and out of the elevator stepped one of the most precious old saints of God, Brother Ernie. My dad was so embarrassed he turned a hundred shades of red. He was trying to hide behind the wheelchair and praying to turn into a fly on the wall. Then it looked as though all the blood ran out of his face and he turned white as a ghost, bald head and all. Then he started trying to explain to Brother Ernie why he was dressed this way and he was stuttering for the right words, but there was just no way to explain it. You would have just had to be there. It was hilarious and we all had a good belly-laugh about it. Brother Ernie thought it was great that he had gone to such extremes to get me out of that hospital bed and back to the land of the living. There has to be a light side to cancer and that was definitely a lighter moment. Laughter is good medicine.

I had gone thirty-three days with no food and finally I was offered some Jell-o. Jell-o never looked so good! It was red, cold and delicious. I was gulping it down and another cancer patient, Lacie, came by my room with some friends to visit for a while. I kept gulping and they kept talking. Whenever Lacie would have visitors she would bring them to my room and visit with me, and whenever I had visitors I would do the same for her. We shared friends, dreams, and our fears. That day as she and her friends were there visiting with me, I began to feel my lips swelling up bigger and bigger. I just laid there with my hand over my mouth until they left.

My mom came in and started yelling for the nurse. Nurse Chuck was taking care of me that day and he came running in the room and his eyes got wider than my mom's and he said, "What have I done? I did not do that! Those are the biggest lips I ever saw!" Later we discovered that the Jell-o was strawberry and I am allergic to strawberries! I had been so excited to get Jell-o that I never thought to ask what kind it was. So, once again, we all had a good laugh and I remembered the word of the Lord, "A merry heart doeth good like a medicine" (Proverbs 17:22 KJV). Whatever storms you are going through, don't forget to laugh. Take a time out and breathe. Remember, God is in control of every situation.

I survived radiation. God delivered me and I survived another five months of chemo after that. Then I heard the words I had prayed to hear for so long, "You are in remission." What a wonderful day in my life! I was alive, I had survived and I was not addicted to any medication! God had delivered me from the storm. The doctors gave me little hope, but "with men this is impossible, but with God all things are possible" (Matthew 19:26 KJV). There were times I questioned if I was going to survive or die. I never feared dying because "to be absent from the body is to be present with the Lord" (II Corinthians 5:8 KJV). Heaven will be a perfect place for rest, joy, happiness, and contentment. It is a place where cancer can never enter. It is our hope of a better day. I found comfort in God's word and in prayer. He is truly my best friend and He wants to be yours, too. He never left my side, just like He promised me. "I will never leave thee, nor forsake thee" (Hebrews 13:5 KJV). God keeps His promises.

In the midst of my chemo and radiation treatments God was always with me. I remember those days, nights, and months and I know that He carried me. The treatments and drugs left me feeble – physically, mentally, and spiritually. When I was weak God was strong. Late at night when everyone was sleeping, He would stand by my bedside and we would weep together. When the morphine clouded my thoughts, He would sit beside me and talk with me, and when I was weary and restless He would sing to me softly, "through many dangers, toils and snares, I have already come; tis grace that bro't me safe thus far, and grace will lead me home" (Amazing Grace). He ministered to me in the stillness of the night. I would open my eyes in the morning light and He was there. A still small voice would say, "be still and know that I am God." I trusted Him and He delivered me over and over again. "The Lord is my strength and song, and He is become my salvation" (Exodus 15:2 KJV).

One realizes how important family ties and friendships are when one is faced with cancer. I have been so blessed to have a loving family and faithful friends. I could have never survived months of chemo and radiation without their love, help, and support. My mom would read to me from God's word and it would bring me such comfort. "Pleasant words are as honeycomb, sweet to the soul, and health to the bones" (Proverbs 16:24 KJV). Dad would never let me give up even though there were many days I could have. He tried so hard to wear that smile no matter what. My younger brother Spencer was just a little trooper through it all. I wanted to be strong for him because he was trying so hard to be strong for me. There was a time when I came home from the hospital and he slept at the foot of my bed in case I needed anything during the night; he was afraid no one would hear me call out. The phone calls, cards, and love offerings poured in on a daily basis. God sent so many special angels to help me and I could never mention them all, but God knows who they are. "A friend loveth at all times" (Proverbs 17:17). In the good and the bad a true friend will always be there. I found out that I have many friends and God has blessed me with a precious church family. It is an honor to be a part of the family of God.

That was the worst year of my life. I felt like a tornado had swept me up and twisted me inside-out for twelve months. It was over and I had survived. What a precious sixteenth birthday present! I rejoiced in my Lord. He had given me back my life and He had changed my way of thinking and my way of preaching. I knew deep down in my heart that I would preach again, and I did. I was more compassionate, understanding, and sympathetic of others and the storms they were weathering. Everything happens for a reason and I knew that in my heart. "To every thing there is a season, and a time to every purpose under Heaven" (Ecclesiastes 3:1) I had been brought low and humbled. Before the cancer I would stand and preach boldly and almost with no compassion, but now I had been given another opportunity to reach out to a world that needed Jesus. Now when I stand to preach it is easy to cry and repeat the words, "God is love, God is love and He loves you. No matter what you've done, He still loves you." God showed me that the only way to win someone to Him is to do it through love. I look back now and before the cancer I would read in the word of God and I thought I knew exactly what the scripture was talking about, but I really did not comprehend a lot of His teachings and promises until my faith had been tested in an extraordinary way. My faith was the one thing I held on to for those twelve months. I knew in my heart if I let go of my faith that I would not survive. I can honestly say, "I have fought a good fight, I have finished my course, I have kept the faith." My God kept His promises.

Chapter 3

The Tropical Storm

Tropical storms are usually named after men and women. They have names like Hugo, Opal, Fredrick, and Andrew. They are severe storms and, when they hit land, sometimes they turn into hurricanes and destroy everything in their path. These bad boys always leave their mark.

In the year 2000 I came face to face with many storms. They were not named after men and women – they had names like cancer, chemo, radiation, and divorce. Each one affected me in a different way. The cancer was physically and spiritually challenging, but my parents' divorce in 2000 was the hardest mental challenge that I had ever faced.

Cancer puts an enormous amount of stress on a family and my family was no exception. Sure we had our problems before the cancer – all families do – but battling cancer created a whole new stress that we had never been faced with. All of a sudden we were on a runaway train. Emotionally, we were all dizzy and a little crazy. Our lives revolved around cancer every moment of every day. We each handled it in different ways. I think if we were given another chance we would handle it with a different attitude. Anxieties and fears can overcome a person. My folks had financial burdens: their jobs, the church, their son who had cancer, and their healthy son who needed them, as well. I think my parents neglected themselves and each other, and not because they meant to, but because they put their children first. Their number-one priority became me and cancer. The fight, the battle to beat cancer, it takes every ounce of strength that you have, whether you are the patient, the parent, or the sibling. It drained the life out of us as a family. Emotions were high all the time and we were all growing weary and tired from the fight. Something would happen, tempers would flare, and someone would say something hurtful. The sad thing about letting all those emotions out before you try to sit and talk about them calmly is that once you have said or done something, you can't take it back. You can apologize one hundred times but the hurt will always be there.

The Devil loves it when the family is struggling and he will use every resource to destroy your home. He is the enemy and he has power to destroy if we allow him. It is so important to stay focused on Jesus, especially when the storms are raging in your life.

Cancer was not the reason my parents divorced, but it enlarged the gulf between them. If your family is facing storms, there are Christian counselors who can help you. My brother and I found help at the Harbor Center, thanks to Children's Hospital. Let me encourage you to talk about the little things, because if you don't they will eventually become big issues. Allow the anger, bitterness, and fear to surface so you can deal with the demons that are trying to destroy you and your family. Keep a positive mindset and keep the Devil out of your home. Stay focused on Jesus; don't take your eyes off Him, even for a minute.

My home was torn apart, my heart was broken, and once again I sat helplessly in the shadow of His cross. I could just see the Devil laughing at me and saying, "Ha, ha, I won this round." He probably thought I would just throw up my hands and quit, but I didn't. I had to realize that I still had a dad, a mom and a brother; we just did not share the same home anymore. It did not help or simplify things in my life, it just made everything more complicated. I had my moments of depression. The adjustment was hard for me and my brother. We no longer had that security blanket called "home." We lived in two houses with people that we loved in each house, but it was never the same.

Our mental health is important to our physical and spiritual health: they all work together. If you allow negative thoughts to consume your mind all the time, then eventually you will become a negative person and that will affect your physical and spiritual well-being. I had to train myself to think positive thoughts, and I did that by reading God's word, praying, meditating on things of God and not giving the Devil any space. If the Devil can rob your thoughts, then he can destroy your peace of mind. We have the power to overcome the tropical storms of life. That power comes from God.

Romans 8:31 KJV:

"If God be for us, who can be against us?"

Romans 8:35 KJV:

"Who shall separate us from the love of Christ?"

Romans 8:37 KJV :

"We are more than conquerors through Him that loved us."

I felt a lot of guilt, and sometimes I blamed myself for the divorce. If I hadn't got sick, if I hadn't got cancer, then maybe my parents could have worked through their differences and kept the home together. Eventually God helped me to come to terms with the fact that it wasn't my fault. Sometimes things happen – people change and we have no control over that. Someone once said that dying would be easier than going through a divorce; I can understand that. You feel like a thief broke into the home and robbed you of every precious thing in your life. Cancer robbed me physically; divorce robbed me mentally; but nothing could rob my relationship with God unless I allowed it to. I read in God's word from the book of *Psalms*, "But David encouraged himself in the Lord his God." I, too, encouraged myself in the Lord my God. I finally gave it all to Jesus and He helped me and strengthened me.

Jesus is the master of the sea. He can speak peace and everything is calm again. Once again I depended on Him completely to help me through, and He did. Do you know Jesus? My prayer is that you will come to know Him and love Him because He cares for you. Do not ride the waves of life without Him because, if you do, you will surely drown in your sorrows. Storms will come – some mild, and some severe – that will leave their mark on you forever.

Eventually, that storm, too, calmed down and both my parents remarried and tried to start a new life for themselves. No matter what a person does, you must be able to forgive and forget. That is what Jesus did with our sins: He forgave us and forgot the sin, and we, too, should strive to be more like that.

Mom and Dad both seem happier than they've ever been. Mom married one of the nicest guys in the world. His name is Mark and he is the best thing that ever happened to her. He is very calm and collected about everything – this man never yells. He has been a help to me and I love him and appreciate all that he has given up for me. Dad, too, remarried. Her name is Kelly and she is a gentle spirit. Kelly is a nurse at Children's Hospital in Birmingham. She has been the sweetest caregiver. She is always reassuring me and I find comfort through her because she has the gentleness and compassion that a nurse should have. She is very soft-spoken and that is comforting when you are facing chemo, radiation, and death.

Whatever is broken, God can mend it. Satan had me convinced that my whole world was going to cave in on me and that I would not survive, but I did. Once again, I walked out of the valley, hand-in-hand with Jesus.

Is your home broken? Is your heart shattered into a million pieces? Do the tears roll uncontrollably down your face? There is a home in Heaven, and nothing ever gets broken there. Life is full of broken dreams and disappointments, but I have good

news: there is a better day ahead. You can overcome! I did!

Chapter 4

Happy Birthday To Me

My battle with cancer began in the spring of 2000. One year later I was in remission. What a wonderful sixteenth birthday present! I felt like a newborn baby and this was the first day of the rest of my life. I was a survivor; I had overcome the storm; I celebrated life. All glory and honor was given to my Lord for the miracle He had given me: the miracle of life.

I had no idea how God was opening up opportunities in my life. My telephone was ringing non-stop day and night. The word was out that I was in remission and that God had performed a miracle in my life. My Lord had delivered me from my afflictions. Psalms 34:19 KJV: "Many are the afflictions of the righteous, but the Lord delivereth them out of all them all."

People were calling me that I did not even know. I had invitations to preach and give my testimony at many schools and churches all across Alabama, Tennessee, Georgia, and Mississippi. The American Cancer Society and the Sunshine Kids asked me to speak at fund-raisers and black-tie affairs. I was given the opportunity to mentor to younger cancer patients at Children's Hospital. I have met and shook the hand of our president. God had opened a door of opportunity and the requests came flooding in. I was so honored and humbled by it all. I remember in the book of II Timothy 4:5 KJV: "but watch thou in all things, endure afflictions, do the work of an evangelist, make full proof of thy ministry." I was amazed at how God had broadened my territory. I stand amazed that I am a child of the King. I would never turn down an invitation and I never got tired of telling about my Savior and all He done for me. God had given me back my life and I would never be able to repay Him for that. All He asked of me was to go out and preach the gospel. Truthfully for the first time in my life God was receiving the glory and honor that was due Him. He is worthy of my praise!

II Samuel 22:4:

"I will call on the Lord, who is worthy to be praised."

II Samuel 22:7 KJV:

"In my distress I called upon the Lord, and cried to my God: and He did hear my voice out of His temple, and my cry did enter into His ears."

I always loved God and I tried to live for Him, but I never understood the depth of His love and the sacrifice of the cross until I suffered great pain and endured many afflictions. I had to decrease so that He could increase in my life. John 3:30-31 KJV says, "He must increase, but I must decrease. He that cometh from above is above all: he that is of the Earth is earthly, and speaketh of the Earth: he that cometh from Heaven is above all."

Has God brought you through a raging storm? Has God helped you to overcome and endure hard times? Have you stopped and taken time to give Him praise for the blessings in your life? He desires praise from your lips. Do you go to the sanctuary of God on the holy Sabbath and worship Him? He is worthy of your praise. Psalms 150: 6 KJV: "Let every thing that hath breath praise the Lord. Praise ye the Lord."

The Lord allowed me to share my testimony with many people and He allowed me to see the fruits of my labor. Souls were won to Christ and the discouraged were encouraged. How good our God is! He did not have to spare my life, but He did. Don't let the storms take away your joy, God will help you; just ask Him.

My hair grew back, I gained weight, I could eat, sleep, preach, play baseball, and do anything else my heart desired. I took nothing for granted in the year 2001. I cherished each and every day. I felt like a butterfly who had finally matured and escaped from the cocoon. I was sailing on a calm sea and a gentle breeze was blowing in my face. I had survived with Jesus and the storm was calm.

Chapter 5

Attitude & Endurance

My entire life I have heard that attitude is everything and now I believe that statement. When I woke up each day facing radiation or chemo treatments I had a choice: I could either have a good attitude or a bad one. I eventually came to the reality that it was much easier to face the treatments with a positive attitude than a negative one. I could have easily chosen to die rather than to live, and I could have just perished in my self-pity rather than tolerate the treatments. As I reflect back on everything I had to bear and suffer, it was a lot easier on the days I had a good outlook. I would wake in the mornings, smile and pray for a good attitude and God would put a smile on my face and comfort in my soul.

In the word of God, in the book of *Second Timothy*, the scripture says, "Thou, therefore, my son, be strong in the grace that is in Christ Jesus. And the things that thou hast heard of me among many witnesses, the same commit thou to faithful men, who shall be able to teach others. Thou, therefore, endure hardness, as a good soldier of Jesus Christ."

During all my sufferings I was constantly reminded of the sufferings of Jesus and I would think to myself, He has suffered so much more than I ever will and He did it because He loved me. He suffered a cruel death on an old rugged cross because He loved me. I want to be a faithful soldier of His cross. I want to always stay in the battle no matter how close I come to the enemy. Whatever my lot I will bear my cross because my Lord has strengthened me and caused me to endure. I have endured and remained faithful to God, and I have continued in the faith. "But he that shall endure unto the end, the same shall be saved" (Matthew 24:13 KJV). "Beareth all things, believeth all things, hopeth all things, endureth all things" (I Corinthians 13:7 KJV).

Don't be misled to believe that the enemy of the cross, the old Devil, did not try to entangle me in his traps and snares. He is the adversary and he will do anything to confuse, destroy, and rob me of my peace of mind. Everyday he worked overtime trying to discourage me and give me a bad attitude. He would whisper in my ear constantly, "You are losing this battle; you will never endure; you will never overcome; you cannot win this battle." Honestly, sometimes I could almost hear him laughing at me. Then I would remember what King David wrote in the book of Psalms 37:12,13 KJV: "The wicked plotteth against the just, and gnasheth upon him with his teeth. The Lord shall laugh at him, for he seeth that his day is coming." I will have the last laugh. My Lord and I will laugh in Heaven while eternity rolls on and the wicked one burns in his own fire forever.

Keep your head up. Smile even when you don't want to. Have a good attitude. Endure the hard times with laughter. You can overcome! You can be victorious in the battle. Life is all about attitude!

We can endure all things with Jesus. He will sustain us, carry us, remain with us, tolerate us, and suffer with us. He loves us! He is the reason I endured with a good attitude. He only asks one thing of you and that is to abide in Him. Stay with Jesus, love Him, read His word, live for Him, share His love with others and he will be there during the storms of life. He will love you more than your own family and friends. He will be your best friend and He will put sunshine in your life on a cloudy day. Storm clouds will roll, thunder will roar, lightning will strike, and the floods will come in your life; be ready for them. Face them with Jesus right by your side. Hold your head up, even when your hair falls out!

Chapter 6

Test of Faith

It was the spring of 2002 and we were playing baseball in the county tournament. I had been experiencing some back pain for several weeks, but I just blamed in on a fender-bender that had occurred in April. When I came up to bat, took a swing, the pain was so excruciating in my back that, for a minute, it took my breath.

Routine x-rays showed nothing, and then, after a series of tests at Children's Hospital, I found myself faced with that dreadful word again, "cancer." It was back with a vengeance. There was a tumor that had grown in the spinal cord canal and it was pushing against a vertebra, causing the vertebra to split. Basically, my back was broken. Before I could blink an eye I was on my way to have radiation treatments again. I had two weeks of radiation and then I started right back on chemo. I was told that I would be on chemo for the rest of my life. Once again I found myself in the middle of a raging storm.

I had always been fascinated with storms and thought that maybe after my baseball career that I might actually pursue a career in meteorology or even become a storm tracker. I was learning a lot about storms and how they toss you out of control. Everything happened so fast this time and I was already educated on terms like "chemo," "radiation," and "pain control." After the initial shock wore off I tried to just accept the fact. I was told that most patients do not survive rhabdomyosarcoma twice. I admit the fear was back and I was dreading the battle.

I had a long heart-to-heart talk with God. My feelings were hurt that He had allowed this to happen again. Did I question Him? Of course I did; He had given me another great year and I did not want to face this dreadful disease again. Cancer robs your happiness if you let it. I kept thinking, "Stay calm, stay focused on Jesus, have a good attitude. You can do this, Cliff." Over and over I tried to convince myself that everything would be ok. God had delivered me once and He would deliver me again.

Dr. Watts and I sat down and had a very realistic conversation about the fact of the matter. The facts were very grim: I had a slim chance of surviving and there was a possibility I could end up in a wheelchair if I did survive. Dr. Watts had to leave the country and he was expecting me to be very weak and close to death by the time he returned to the States. Well, guess what? The folks on Sand Mountain and all the surrounding areas began to pray and call out my name to God. I love this little mountain and everybody here. The Bible-Belt is just a circle of praying people who believe in God and His power to save and heal. We are many denominations, many different ages, and our beliefs differ, but one thing is the same, we worship one God, the only true God. Many saints cried out to God on my behalf and He heard their cries. "If ye have faith as a grain of mustard seed, ye shall say unto this mountain, Remove hence to yonder place; and it shall remove; and nothing shall be impossible unto you" (Matthew 17:20 KJV). Have you ever seen a mustard seed? They are so tiny you can barely see them at all. I had faith, Sand Mountain had faith, the Bible-Belt had faith, my family and friends from all over the States had that same faith, and it worked!

God continued to strengthen and heal my body day after day. When Doctor Watts came home, he was amazed to see me doing so well. That was a great day and I shall never forget it. I felt like, that very moment, when our eyes met, that my faith and his became much stronger. We rejoiced together.

God touched me and healed me again. The chemo was working and the cancer was shrinking. Eventually, the pain vanished. God required some things of me and that was to honor Him and glorify Him in all that I did. He was using my life, my testimony, and my journey to receive praise from my lips. He delivered me so I could share the miracle with all of you. God is awesome and I love Him with my whole heart! I owe Him everything I have. Everyday I was refreshed and strengthened by the hand of God. I felt the prayers as the saints prayed. I had overcome another storm.

This miracle reminded me of another miracle that happened over 2000 years ago to a man named Lazarus. Pick up your Bible and read in the book of *John*, chapter 11. The man had died, been dead for four days, and his family sent for Jesus to come. When Jesus arrived at the home of Lazarus, his sister was upset because the Lord had tarried His coming. Jesus said unto them, "if thou wouldest believe, thou shouldest see the glory of God." Then Jesus spoke these words, "Lazarus, come forth," and the man came forth from the dead. Many who witnessed believed on Jesus that day. Earlier in the same story, Jesus spoke these words, "This sickness is not unto death, but for the glory of God, that the Son of God might be glorified thereby." I can relate to this story because the hand of God touched me and prevented me from death... again. Praise be to the Lamb of God! Oh, how sweet to trust in Jesus! I shall never forget all that the Lord has done for me and all the raging storms He has calmed in my life. All glory is due Him and I shall praise Him with my mouth until the day I leave this place to go where He is.

I will admit it has been a long, hard journey. I have been broken into a million pieces. My heart, my spirit, my dreams were all shattered. When I was at one of my lowest points, a friend sent me this poem. I want to share it with you in hopes that it will encourage you as it encouraged me time after time.

Chosen Vessel– (Author Unknown)

The master was searching for a vessel to use.

On the shelf there were many; which one would he choose?

Take me, cried the gold one, I'm shiny and bright.

I'm of great value and I do things just right.

My beauty and luster will outshine the rest,

And for someone like you, master, gold would be the best.

The Master passed on with no word at all.

He looked at a silver urn, narrow and tall.

I'll serve you, dear Master, I'll pour out your wine,

And I'll be at your table whenever you dine.

My lines are so graceful, my carvings so true,

And my silver will always compliment you.

Unheeding, the Master passed on to the brass.

It was wide-mouthed and shallow, and polished like glass.

Here! Here! Cried the vessel, I know I will do.

Place me on your table for all men to view.

Look at me, called the goblet of crystal so clear.

My transparency shows my contents so dear.

Though fragile am I, I will serve you with pride,

And I'm sure I'll be happy in your house to abide.

The master came next to a vessel of wood.

Polished and carved, it solidly stood.

You may use me, dear Master, the wooden bowl said,

But I'd rather you used me for fruit, not for bread.

Then the Master looked down and saw a vessel of clay.

Empty and broken it helplessly lay.

No hope had the vessel that the Master might choose,

To cleanse and make whole, to fill and to use.

Ah! This is the vessel I've been hoping to find.

I will mend it and use it and make it all mine.

I need not the vessel with pride of itself,

Nor the one who is narrow to sit on the shelf,

Nor the one who is bigmouthed and shallow and loud,

Nor the one who displays his contents so proud,

Not the one who thinks he can do all things just right,

But this plain earthly vessel filled with my power and might.

Then gently he lifted the vessel of clay,

Mended and cleansed it and filled it that day,

Spoke to it kindly, there is work you must do.

Just pour out to others as I pour into you.

God picked up my broken heart, broken spirit, and broken dreams and He mended me into a vessel that He could use. Are you broken? God can mend you back together; He mended me many times and He will do the same for you because He loves you. Is there something God is asking you to do? Are you afraid of failure, defeat, or embarrassment? Remember this, "If God brings you to it, He will bring you through it! Being confident of this very thing, that he which hath begun a good work in you will perform it until the day of Jesus Christ" (Philippians 1:6 KJV).

In the word of God in the book of *Jeremiah*, God spoke to Jeremiah and told him to go down to the potter's house. While Jeremiah was at the potter's house he watched as the potter wrought a work on the wheels, and the word of the Lord came to him, saying, "O house of Israel, cannot I do with you as this potter?" saith the Lord. "Behold, as the clay is in the potter's hand, so are ye in mine hand, O house of Israel." Just allow God to mold you and work a good work through you.

You never know how many lives you may touch and how God will use that life to

touch another. Remember, "I can do all things through Christ which strengtheneth

me" (Philippians 4:13 KJV – thanks, Jess!). Don't be afraid; just step out on faith;

faith can move mountains, calm the sea, and chase away the Devil!

Chapter 7

Things Are Not Always What They Seem

It was August 31, 2002, the first football game of the season and everyone was excited. It was our senior year and I was just happy to be alive and be able to share this moment. I had just been released from the hospital earlier in the day and I was very tired and washed out, but my spirit was high. I sat in the middle of all these energetic people anticipating a wonderful night with friends and family. It was almost game time and I kept looking for Sarah. Sarah was a beautiful, energetic cheerleader and she was never late for anything, and I had become concerned because she was not there. Shortly the news began to spread that she and another cheerleader had been in a horrible car accident. I made a couple of phone calls and quickly it was confirmed. She had been air-lifted to Huntsville Hospital. I just couldn't believe this was happening. It only takes a minute for our lives to be turned upside-down.

The spirit of God spoke to my heart and said, "Go." I made a phone call and left the football stadium to go and be with Sarah and her family. That drive over to Huntsville seemed to take forever and I felt an urgency to hurry and get there. Sarah had dedicated her life to God and she was trying so hard to be pleasing to Him. I kept thinking there had to be a purpose and a reason for this accident. As I silently prayed, God gave me a peace that she would be all right. My body was tired from chemo that week but God strengthened me and allowed me to make the trip. When we walked in, we were greeted by family, friends, and Brother Gary, the pastor of the church where Sarah attended. I was allowed to go into ICU. I held her hand and prayed for the healing touch of God. It broke my heart, the sight that I saw. She was so lifeless and helpless. Only the healing power of God could save her. God strengthened us both that night. I was a survivor, and Sarah would be, too. Slowly the miracles in Sarah's life began to unfold. She was in a coma for four days and God began to work. Everyone was amazed that she had survived. Sarah had a fractured pelvis, basal skull fracture, burst eardrum, and six-nerve palsy. Her body slowly began to heal. After twelve weeks in the hospital and two weeks of rehab she was on her way back to a normal life. What a miracle! God was given glory for it all. What a testimony this young lady has! Many lives were touched through her ordeal. My God is bigger than anything! Everything that happens, happens for a reason.

Sarah was beautiful, smart, athletic, and had her whole life ahead of her. It would have been easy to ask God why this happened to her. I have found that bad things happen to good people and that is just the way it is.

The day Sarah got out of the hospital was our homecoming football game and she was able to be there (on crutches). That same day I was given an opportunity to give my testimony to a group of young people from a Children's Home. I remember standing in front of these children of all ages and seeing the pain in their eyes. I asked the question, "Lord what have these children been through, what hard times have they endured, and what kind of storms are raging in their lives?" As I began to speak all I could do was tell them how much Jesus loved them and that sometimes bad things happen to good people. These young people did not ask for the hurt and disappointments in their lives. They probably thought that bad things happened to them because they were bad people. That is just a lie of the Devil. Hard times will come to us all, but there is a God in Heaven who loves us and will help us to overcome those trying times.

That evening a young lady sitting on the front row began to cry as I began to tell them about the love of God, and I knew in my heart that my spirit had connected with hers. I had no way of knowing about the broken promises and broken dreams in her young life, but I did know that Jesus was there for her and he always would be. I hope that she realized it that night, also. We do not have to face anything alone. God opened my eyes a little wider that day. He allowed me to hurt with those who hurt and to weep with those who weep. "Rejoice with them that do rejoice, and weep with them that weep" (Romans 12:15 KJV). My journey has made me more compassionate and more understanding of others and the battles they are fighting.

I am a survivor; Sarah is a survivor; those children from the home are survivors; and you can survive, also.

Cancer has not been all doom and gloom. God has allowed me to use it to bring glory and honor to Him. The death angel could have taken me many times but God said, "Not yet." There are some things that cancer cannot do. I found this on a bookmark when I stayed at the Hope Lodge in Birmingham. It says: "Cancer can not cripple love, shatter hope, erode faith, rob me of my peace, destroy my confidence, shut out my memories, silence my courage, invade my soul, reduce eternal life, quench the spirit, or lessen the power of the resurrection." God is love, He is hope, peace, confidence, courage, and eternal life and cancer can not take that away from me. My Lord does all things well. He has walked with me every step of the way and He will keep me until the day my journey ends.

43

Cancer has opened many opportunities in my life. I have endured and overcome many obstacles. Don't look at me and think that cancer has been a curse from God; it has been just the opposite. In many ways it has been a blessing, because it allowed me to meet some wonderful people and to witness to thousands of the love of God. It is a heavy cross to carry, but I will carry it with pride because it is my cross to bear. I want to be a friend to Jesus because He has been a friend to me. He went to Calvary and died a cruel death so that we may have eternal life. He could have called the angels to come and rescue Him, but He didn't. He carried His cross all the way and I will carry mine. This bitter cup will someday pass from me, but until it does I will drink it.

What is your bitter cup to drink? How heavy is your cross today? Sure, it would be easier to give up than to press onward, but out there somewhere, somebody needs you. You can make a difference in someone's life. The Devil will tell you that you are nothing and worthless, but he is a liar. Jesus needs disciples, young and old, to spread the word that Jesus saves.

"Both young men and maidens; old men and children; Let them praise the name of the Lord: for His name alone is excellent; His glory is above the Earth and Heaven" (Psalms: 148:12-13 KJV). We all have a place in the kingdom of God. There is a work for you to do regardless of your age or your status in life. There is work for all to do. Take your part and be the best you can be. Give it all to Jesus. Surrender heart, mind, body, and soul. I promise it will be worth selling out to Him.

The Scrapbook

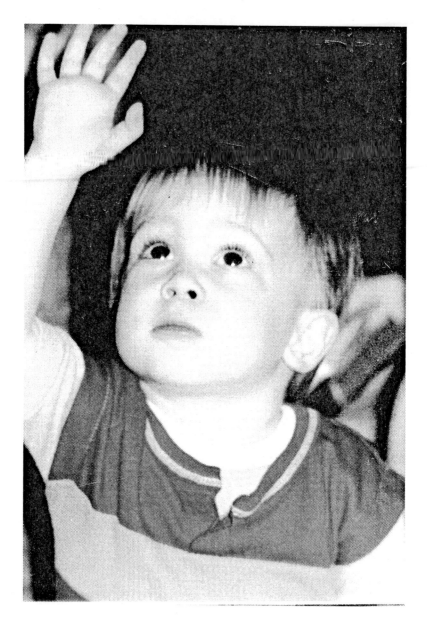

Praising God at Bible School (18 months old)

Kindergarten Graduation (5 years old)

Baseball Dreams

Preached first sermon at 12 years old. (Cliff & Spencer)

The Scrapbook

Ribbon-cutting at Sardis High School.

In Remission! (16 years old)

Boaz Middle School had a penny drop and raised $5000.00 for Cliff and his

family.

Cliff, with Anna Spruiell and Principal Landers.

Cliff meets President Bush in 2001.

(Thanks to The Sunshine Kids.)

Valentine's Day at dear old Sardis High.

(Cliff with Mrs. Bryant and Mrs. Mashburn)

The Scrapbook

Cliff receives $1000.00 Scholarship from The American Cancer Society.

(Front row – Kelly, Spencer, Kathy, Mark. Back row – Greg, Cliff, Stella, Jim, &

Shaun.)

Cliff with brother Spencer.

The Cruise – 2003.

Cliff & Sarah – Prom 2003

(Soul-Mates)

Friends – Prom 2003

(Bobby, Josh, & Cliff)

The Scrapbook

Homecoming 2002

Queen – Misha Langley & King – Cliff Jacobs

Sardis High School – Awards Night

"The Survivors"

(Bobby, Sarah, & Cliff)

Graduation – May 2003

Cliff accepting diploma from Principal Beard.

Cliff & Sara at Disney World

August 2003

Living the busy life of a teen and growing up in the twenty-first century, I never took the time to look around and truly appreciate what God has made for us to enjoy. In the past I normally took a vacation once a year to the mountains to look around in the shops and watch the people. Then, toward the end of 2002, I was asked if I had ever done much hunting, and all I could say was I had never taken the time. A friend asked me to set aside a Saturday and go with him to the woods. I did and there I found myself alone with nature.

For once in my life I felt like an actual part of the beautiful creation and plan of God. That one hunting trip has since turned into an infatuation. I am an avid and consistent hunter who has recently harvested my first deer. After deer season I hope to go turkey hunting and maybe even dove hunting.

Some ask what drives me to come back hunting. To their surprise it is not the actual excitement of the kill that makes me want to keep coming back, but the feeling I get when I am alone in the woods with God and nature. To experience wildlife in its natural habitat is awesome. I am glad my friend talked me into going. Hunting is an activity that I want to pass down to my son when I have children.

"The Hunt"

2003

Chapter 8

The Class of 2003

I remember when I was first diagnosed with cancer, thinking, how will my classmates react? Will they look at me like I'm weird? Will they treat me differently? Will I lose the friends I've come to know and love over the years? Anxiety eats away at your mind when you come face-to-face with your demons.

When the news got back to school that I had cancer, I was amazed at the support I received from the entire school, and especially the class of 2003. The cancer actually brought us closer together; we formed a bond that could never be broken. I really don't understand why, but our class had a lot of obstacles to overcome. I wasn't the only one who had fought for his life: one classmate had been in a freak accident and was run over by a trailer; another one was in a horrible car accident; and many others suffered from different situations in their lives. As I reflect back now I can see how God was pulling us all closer together. I would have to say that our class was just one big family: whenever one hurt, we all hurt. I think that God was preparing us for the future that lies in front of us. I believe that we are all strong, and we are all survivors because of the love and compassion we had one for another.

My classmates wrapped me in their love and support. We laughed together and cried together. I could have never made it without those guys. When I was diagnosed they started wearing white ribbons to show they cared and that they were pulling for me. They raised money, bought a huge white ribbon, and placed it around a large tree in front of the school. They had fund-raisers to help my family financially; they sent care packs, cards, and prayers. When I was declared in remission in 2001, I cut the ribbon from the tree, symbolizing a new day and another chance at life. We all rejoiced that day. It is a day I will never forget. Later that year the yearbook staff held a dedication ceremony to dedicate a page in the annual to me. I was so touched. The entire school helped to nurture me back to health that year. Whenever I was having a bad day, one of them would call or stop by and my spirits would be lifted. They always included me in everything and that was important to me. I missed a lot of school and I needed to feel like I still had a place there. Love can move mountains and build bridges. The power of love is an awesome thing.

When the cancer returned, so did the encouragement and support from Sardis High

School. They are the best! I missed a lot of school during my battle with cancer

and there were days I wanted to just quit because I was so tired and worn down,

but someone would always come along and give me a gentle push – sometimes my

parents or my classmates, but always Aunt Stella. Aunt Stella is my dad's sister,

and she teaches at Sardis. She was determined that I would keep my grades up,

graduate, and attend college in the fall.

My senior year came and went so quickly. I was in the hospital more than I was

out. Looking back I praise God because He allowed me to be a part of special

events such as Homecoming, Carnation Ball, Senior Prom, and, on May 22, 2003,

I graduated with honors. I had lived to accomplish many things that were important

to me and I did this by the grace of God, and with the help of my friends.

So often we just forget to tell those we love how special they are. I wish we could

have all spent more quality time together. I felt their love and prayers every day. I

could close my eyes and see their smiling faces and hear their laughter. I pray that

the bond we have will never be broken.

We will all start a new journey now as we part and go our own way. Our lives will take different directions and we will pursue different careers, but we will always be a circle of friends who fought cancer together. I will remember them always.

To all the Sardis High School graduating class of 2003, thank you from the bottom of my heart, and may God bless you all. I love you guys; you are the best! Wherever you go, whatever you do, remember me being happy when I was with you. My prayer is that you will all come to know God and accept Jesus as your personal savior. I am going to a place soon where there is no pain, no tears, no cancer, and no goodbyes. My wish is that you will all come there someday and our circle will once again be complete.

Friends are blessings from God – don't take them for granted, because life is short. Thanks for the laughter.

Chapter 9

Thoughts of Suicide

When you read the title of this chapter you probably said to yourself, no way would he even think about that! Why not? I am human just like everyone else, and trust me, there were days I thought about it... days I planned it. Sometimes the troubles of life build a wall around us and we cannot see outside the wall. Many times Satan would play mind games with me and have me convinced that I had no reason to live and that I should just end it. Don't you think for one minute just because you are a born-again Christian, strong in the faith, trusting God daily, that the old Devil has no power. Friend, he does have power and we struggle with him daily. You know his job is to get inside our heads and convince us that we are nobodies. He loves to stir up trouble for the children of God and he will sneak into our lives at the times we are low in spirit and try to devour and destroy us.

Chemo, radiation, pain medication, and a broken home can cause you to be angry, depressed, weak in body, mind, and spirit. The hard times make you want to throw up your hands and quit. Every time that I would think about suicide, God would bring scripture to mind, such as the story of Jonah. Jonah was very angry and he prayed to God and said, "Therefore now, O Lord, take, I beseech thee, my life from me; for it is better for me to die than to live" (Jonah 4:3 KJV). Jonah just gave up, but God came on the scene and touched Jonah and strengthened him. Many times God did the same thing for me. Every time I wanted to die, God would whisper in my ear the words he said to Job, "Gird up thy loins now like a man; I will demand of thee, and declare thou unto me" (Job 40:7 KJV). God would reach down in love, pick me up out of my self-pity, and tell me to stop whining. I could just hear him saying, "Cliff Jacobs, get up out of that bed and stand on your feet and go preach the gospel! You have a purpose and I have a plan for you! There is no time to sit around feeling sorry for yourself, there is work to do." So I would pick myself up (by the strength of God) and hold my head high because my Lord had come by my way and Satan had been defeated again. Many times this happened. How precious is the love of God for His children?

The Devil kept telling me time after time that I had nothing left to give. He had me convinced that I had nothing left to offer God and that I was just in the way. I felt like a burden to my parents, and I felt like my little brother had given up so

69

much because of me and cancer. I watched my grandparents' eyes sadden as they saw me withering away. I felt like, if I just died, then it would lift the burden for them all. My Papa Walker was not in good health and I hated that he was having to watch me die. I love him like a father, and he and I share a special bond. It seemed so unfair that he might have to say goodbye to me rather than me saying goodbye to him. Life is not always fair. We expect the old to die before the young, but it doesn't always happen that way. I felt so helpless and useless at times. I remember a story about a widow woman and her son in God's word. The Bible says that there was a man by the name of Elijah and he came to the gate of the city and he saw the woman there and asked her to fetch him a drink of water and a morsel of bread. The widow woman replied, "As the Lord, thy God, liveth, I have not a cake, but an handful of meal in a barrel, and a little oil in a cruse; and, behold, I am gathering two sticks, that I may go in and dress it for me and my son, that we may eat it and die." Then Elijah told the woman to fear not; that the Lord of Israel would supply her with meal and oil for the rest of her days. He did just that. That little woman probably just stood amazed at the grace and mercy of God. I stand amazed every day because of His goodness toward me. I am not worthy to be His child, but He loves me, anyway.

Is your barrel running dry? Do you feel like you just don't have enough strength to carry on? Are you running on empty? Are you hungry and thirsty? Have you given up on life? Well, friend, I have felt all these things and I almost gave up a hundred times. I had almost given up on me and on my life, but I never gave up on God. I knew that He could sustain me and He did, time after time. What a friend we have in Jesus! Don't give up. Don't give in to Satan and the mind games that he is playing with you. Trust Jesus: He never fails. If there is still life, then there is still hope. God has a plan for you and He has a purpose for your life. You are very important to Him and He loves you very much. Remember, He loved you so much that He sent His only son to die a cruel death on an old rugged cross. Friend, that is love.

Don't pull the trigger; don't swallow the pills; don't cut the wrist; don't run that car off that mountain. You are important; you have a purpose in this life! Stop whining; stop having that pity party. Get up and take charge of your life! Look the Devil in the eyes, put your hands on your hips and tell him to get behind you! Somewhere there is somebody who loves you and needs you. Ask Jesus to come into your heart – He will save you. Are you a Christian who has wandered far from God? Come back to Him; He is standing with outstretched arms. You do not have to live a defeated life; there is joy is serving the Lord. He loves you when no one else does; He cares when you feel like no one cares. Jesus is His name. You can be a survivor with Him on your side. I would not have lived to tell this story if He had not sustained me. I am living proof that Jesus cares. By the way, I care, too, and

that is why I am sharing this story with you.

Chapter 10

A Mother's Heart

By: Kathy Fleck

The miracles in our life did not just begin to happen when we started this battle with cancer. When Cliff's dad and I were married and started to talk about having a family, we were told by my doctor that I couldn't have children. Within weeks I found myself pregnant with our first child, Clifford William Jacobs – much to my surprise, and everyone else's. God had sent our first miracle. Little did we know this would be the beginning of many miracles in our life. My life was close to perfect. I was blessed of God. I had two healthy sons, a loving husband, a good home life and a wonderful church family. God had been so good to me and my family. I had no idea that I was about to enter the longest, hardest battle of my life.

Cancer, what a dreadful word! You are never prepared to hear that word, especially when it pertains to your child. I remember the day Cliff had the lump removed from his mouth. Doctor Brown is a very happy spirit and he always makes eye contact when he is speaking with you. He performed the surgery that day. When he finished the procedure he came out in the waiting area to speak with us. I asked him if we had good news and, instead of looking at me he looked up at the ceiling. I felt sick to my stomach. He was very honest with us about the fact that it looked like cancer, but he would not know for sure until the biopsy came back. I lost it for a moment; I was in shock. Our only hope was that he could be wrong, so I held on to my faith, waiting for a telephone call and praying that he was wrong.

The day the call came I was at work. My husband called and spoke with my supervisor. He explained to her that Cliff had cancer and that she should not let me drive home. She asked a minister to be there with me. When I walked into the office and saw him, I knew in my heart what I was about to hear. I picked up the phone and my husband said, "Cliff's got cancer." I just sat there crying and hugging the phone. I had only been an employee there for three weeks and my supervisor was just an angel through it all. I remember her saying to me that day, "Kathy, I'll help you through this." She kept her promise. In the days and months and years to come I would go in and work when I could. Everyone was so supportive and encouraging. They took up love offerings for me and my family. I am so blessed to work with these wonderful people at Medical Data Systems. A heartfelt thanks to them all. They were there to comfort me on that dreadful day in the spring of 2000 and I will never forget their love and concern for me and my family.

The battle, the struggle, the journey had begun. If I could explain the last three years to you, I would have to say it had been like climbing a mountain – a steep mountain. When we would climb up a few hundred feet we would slip and fall back to the bottom. We would dust ourselves off and start climbing again. The furious winds would blow and we would hold on for dear life. Finally we would reach a resting place and we could sit down just for a minute and catch our breath. It wouldn't be very long until we would be hiking back up that mountain, and each step was getting harder. We would lose our grip and back to the bottom we would go. We haven't reached the top of the mountain yet, but we are still climbing and fighting those furious winds.

I remember when I was fifteen years old, I went with my brother-in-law looking for a Christmas tree over on Buffington Road. I geared up with my hiking boots, gloves, and an ax, and we searched until we found that perfect tree. I finally spotted that perfect tree and I wasn't leaving until we had it. It took forever to reach the tree. We were exhausted but we kept climbing until we reached the tree. It was all about determination. I am determined to reach the top of this mountain, someday, just like I was determined to have that perfect Christmas tree.

When a person's life is turned upside-down, many changes take place. When we first found out that Cliff had cancer, I was numb. I wanted it to be me and not him. He was an innocent child and I could not bear the thoughts of him suffering this. I have never been one to have a lot of patience and I find that, through it all, God has taught me patience. In the word of God we are told that tribulation worketh patience. It is true. I had always felt like I was in control of everything until cancer entered into my home. God is in control of everything and we are in control of nothing. My faith in God has become stronger every day. I depend on him for everything. When the troubles and trials of this life overwhelm us and we feel no one is there and that no one understands, God is there with outstretched arms holding out His hands to us.

If I could give any advice to other parents facing this I would tell them to be strong for their children, spend quiet time together reading from God's word, and talk about it. The worst thing you can do is to pretend that it isn't really happening to your family and that it will go away. Be realistic about everything. God will give you grace to face each day. I have learned to put everything in God's hands; try not to carry all those burdens on your own shoulders. Mothers want to protect their children, but I have learned we cannot protect them from everything. Get educated about chemo, radiation, pain medication and the side effects. You need to understand what your child is going through – physically, mentally, and spiritually. Cancer does not just affect the child, it affects the whole family. Talk to a family counselor. Be open and honest about your feelings. You don't have to be brave all the time. It is ok to cry. Let your child know that. Crying cleanses the heart and refreshes the soul.

God sent many precious saints of God to encourage us. There was one day in particular that I had one of those days at work when nothing went right and I was spiritually at a very low spot. I stopped by the mailbox on my way in and there was a card addressed to me and I found that unusual because they were always addressed to Cliff or the Jacobs Family. I opened it and there was a beautiful card about faith. When I opened it up to look inside there was a small pack of mustard seeds. I sat there and held on to that pack of mustard seeds and cried like a baby. I never knew who sent the card because there was no name on it, but God knows and He knew it was just what I needed. I remembered the scripture from God's word, "If ye have faith as a grain of mustard seed, ye shall say unto this mountain, Remove hence to yonder place and it shall remove; and nothing shall be impossible unto you" (Matthew 17:20 KJV). May God bless whoever the angel was that sent the seeds. I found renewed strength and faith that day.

I was asked this question, "If the doctor told me I had one more day with my son, how would I spend that day?" I would play the piano and he would play his guitar, and we would sing praises to God, and then, at the end of that day, I would wrap him in my arms, I would kiss him on the head and tell him that a part of me would go to Heaven with him and that soon we would be together again. Then I would hold on to him until his Father called for him, and when the angels would take him from my arms I would let him go to be with Jesus. I would try to envision him taking his shoes off and walking on that holy ground, that street of gold and sitting down with Jesus, cancer-free.

I wish that I could have taken it from him and suffered it myself. My heart was broken on a daily basis. Watching my son suffer this horrible disease was the most devastating thing I had ever witnessed. My daily prayer is that one day they will find a cure and your sons and daughters will never have to endure the sufferings of cancer. My son was brave and strong through it all. His strength and help came from his Heavenly Father. The only way I survived was through Jesus. My prayers go out to all the other families battling cancer. May you find refuge in the arms of Jesus. No matter how steep that mountain gets, keep climbing; never give up; press onward.

Chapter 11

A Father's Determination

By: Greg Jacobs

The day I received the call that my son had cancer was the darkest day of my life. The sun stopped shining. Cliff was in the shower when the call came in from the doctor. I hung up the phone I went out into the garage and sat down on the door step. I cried out to God and asked why, why my son? I was angry and outraged for a moment, and then I pulled myself together and went back inside to break the news.

He sat down and, as I began to tell him, one tear rolled out of his left eye and trickled down his cheek. After just a brief moment, he said, "I can't lose this battle; if I die, I go home to be with my Heavenly Father, and if I live I stay here with my earthly family. I can't lose, Dad," and this scripture came to us, "Christ shall be magnified in my body, whether it be by life, or by death. For to me to live is Christ

and to die is gain. But if I live in the flesh, this is the fruit of my labor: yet what I

shall choose I wot not. For I am in a strait betwixt two, having a desire to depart,

and to be with Christ; which is far better; Nevertheless to abide in the flesh is more

needful for you" (Philippians 1:20-24 KJV). "For unto you it is given in the behalf

of Christ, not only to believe on Him, but also to suffer for His sake" (Philippians

1:29 KJV). I found strength through his courage. I was trying to be strong for him,

but he was a lot stronger and braver than I was.

That day I purposed in my heart to never give up and to never let Cliff give up. I

would pray for God to keep the fight in us all and He did time after time. Every

time we would think we had won, the cancer would come back. We would get up

and then get knocked back down. It has been a boxing match and we have many

bruises and scars to show for it. The spiritual, physical, and mental strain was

sometimes so overwhelming. We would grow tired and weary and we would have

our moments of tears and feel sorry for ourselves, but then we would pray for God

to strengthen us and He would put the fight back in us all.

Cliff had played baseball all his life and he had been a very disciplined and

dedicated team member. He loved that sport and I believe years of training to be

the best helped him to fight this battle with cancer. I always pushed him to be the best player and to never quit. You can't always hit a home run and you can't always win, but you can be the best you can be. He used those tools while fighting cancer. He fought with all he had; he gave all he had and he never gave up or quit fighting. He will never know how proud I am to be his dad and how proud I am to call him son.

The first round of radiation took a toll on his body and we almost lost him. He was so sick and could not eat or drink anything for many days. The treatment left him so weak and fragile and I was so afraid he might be giving up. I would smile and tell him there was nowhere to quit, because God had brought him too far. I would reassure him that everything was going to be ok; just keep fighting. When he would close his eyes and sleep I would weep because I was growing weary. I knew I could never let him see me worried, weak, or discouraged, so I hid a lot of sorrow behind my smile. I couldn't give up. There were times he probably just wanted me to shut up and go away, but there was no way he was getting rid of me that easily. Sometimes we, as parents, push our children a little too hard and expect a little too much from them. The one thing I knew that brought him comfort was just knowing I was there for him. I did not always have the answer, and sometimes I could not grasp the right words to say to encourage him, but he knew I was there and that I loved him and nothing could change that.

He put on the whole armor of God and he fought like a brave young soldier should. His faith in God increased each time he would overcome another round. Cliff taught me to be a better person and to have more faith in God. He was a fine example of what a Christian should be. I say his name with pride and respect. I let him down many times, but he never let me down. I hope someday I can be half the man that my son was.

If I could offer any advice to other parents going through this, I would tell them to keep fighting; don't ever give up. Stay strong for your child, because they can sense your fears and anxieties, and that will cause them to be overcome with fear. Determine to beat the cancer, don't let it beat you. Laugh often: it is good medicine for you and your child. Take advantage of the days they feel strong and spend quality time doing the things they enjoy. Don't let cancer be the main topic of your everyday life. It will rob you of the little things if you let it. Seize the moment, because every moment is precious.

Chapter 12

My Brother, My Friend

By: Spencer Jacobs

When Cliff was first diagnosed with cancer, I was afraid that he would die. He had to be in the hospital a lot that first year and I had to stay with my grandmother. It was a hard time for the whole family, but we always knew that God was with us. The one thing I have learned from Cliff through it all is that God is in control and we must be strong and brave. I tried to be strong for Cliff and he tried to be strong for me.

During the first year Cliff had to have lots of chemo treatments and he was sick a lot. He had to take lots of pain medicine, and sometimes it would make him feel bad and he was a little grumpy. I learned that you just had to be patient with him and stay out of his way when he was grumpy. I had my grumpy days, too. We all did. You just have to learn that there will be good days and there will be bad days. Even though Cliff had cancer we were still brothers, and we still fussed at each other a lot. Most of all we still loved each other and nothing would change that, not even cancer. We tried to live normal lives, but really, nothing is normal when someone in your family has cancer.

I guess there were times when I felt a little left out and there were things I couldn't participate in at school because Mom and Dad just didn't have the time, but I was never angry about that. I always remembered that my brother was sick and he needed them. I knew they loved me, too, and that would never change. Sometimes you just can't do everything you want to. I have learned that it is better to give than to receive. Cliff needed a lot of care and attention, and I understood that.

There was some days and nights that we were able to stay at the Hope Lodge. It was like an apartment that was close to the hospital. We could all be together for a little while. That was really cool, and I liked it when I got to stay there. Hospitals are not my favorite place to be. Boring, boring, boring. Hope Lodge was more like a home away from home and you could get away from the hospital for a little while.

After the first year, and Cliff was back to normal, I thought it was all behind us. Then, when the cancer came back, I kept thinking, "Here we go again." It didn't seem fair, but I have learned that sometimes life just throws you curveballs. Life has thrown us a lot of curveballs in the past three years. Cancer became our whole life. Everywhere we went people would stop and talk to us about Cliff's cancer. I got really tired of hearing about it all the time. I would just walk away. Sometimes, you just don't want to talk or hear about it.

There is a really cool camp called Camp Smile-A-Mile. It is a summer camp for the siblings of cancer patients – only the siblings. The first time I went was in the summer of 2001. We went swimming, fishing, boating, and many other things. It was so much fun and we didn't have to talk about the cancer, and it was so good to get away from it. It helped me so much. That week was all about me and not about brother's cancer. I made lots of friends there and was able to relax and just have fun. There isn't a lot of fun going on when someone you love has cancer. You take the good days and cherish them and they help you get through the bad days.

Also, there is a place that is connected to Children's Hospital called Children's Harbor. They have counselors who will talk to you and listen to you about any problems that you are having to deal with. They are very sweet and very caring people. It is good to know that there is someone who understands what you are going through. There was this one day that I went there to talk to one of the counselors and we were playing a game and she started asking me questions. I did not want to answer them, so I would suggest we play another game. She quickly caught on that I was just playing mind games with her. I thought it was funny. It is a good place to go and unwind and share your thoughts with someone other than family members. They are very concerned and caring people.

If I could give any advice to another young person who is having to deal with cancer, I would just say to them to stay strong and be brave. Our God will take care of it all. I hope they find a cure soon, so families don't have to go through what my family has gone through. Just remember, cancer can't take away the love, and God is bigger than cancer.

Cliff is more than my brother; he is my friend and we will survive this together. I hope someday I grow up to be as brave as he is. I love him and I know he loves me, and that is important. I hope his story helps someone to keep fighting and never give up.

God is bigger than cancer – Cliff always says that.

Chapter 13

Fear Not

The doctors have told me it is just a matter of time. The cancer has now made its home in my lungs and eventually they will fill up with fluid. My kidneys will shut down or I will drown from the fluid. Sounds frightening. The unknown can unnerve you and cause you to be fearful. In God's word there is a man by the name of Moses, and God had commanded Moses to lead the children of Israel out of Egypt. Moses told the people to fear not, stand still, and see the salvation of the Lord, which He would show to them. He told them that the Egyptians – whom they had seen – would not be seen by them again, anymore. He told them that the Lord would fight for them and that they should hold their peace (Exodus 14:13-14 KJV)

I am sure those people were very frightened of the enemy, just as I am frightened about the sting of death. Those people believed in their God and they had to step out on faith and trust Him. I believe that when death comes to me that I will have enough faith to trust my Lord to deliver me from that sting. My hope is in the Lord Jesus just as those Israelites. The Lord parted the sea and those people walked across on dry land. When death comes to me, the Lord will part the Jordan River and I will walk across on dry land. This fluid in my lungs may drown me or my kidneys may shut down, but I will reach Heaven unharmed and escape the enemy, cancer. I'm living with cancer, not dying with it. My Lord will say when it is time to pass over, not cancer.

I have victory in Jesus. He has fought my battles for me; He has fed me when I was hungry, given me to drink when I was thirsty, and my hope is in Him. We do not have to fear anything with Jesus walking beside us. He will go before us and make a way for us to cross over. God's grace is sufficient, even in death.

It would be easy now to just sit down and give up, but I still have breath in my body. As long as I live I will lift up the name of Jesus. I will preach His word and share His love with anyone who will listen. I owe Him everything. He is the reason I am still alive and He deserves my praise and worship even on my deathbed. I am still getting invitations to come and preach God's word and to give my testimony.

When I have passed from this world to be with Jesus, my hope is that my testimony will live on. I just want everyone out there to know that Jesus is all you need – in good times, bad times, and all the time. He will soon deliver me from cancer and the pain that I have endured. If I had to do it all over again, I would. You see, my reward is going to be awesome! My Father is a king and He owns it all. I will live in a mansion and not have a mortgage payment, utility bills, or homeowner's insurance to pay for. My Father paid for it all. My street will be paved with gold, the walls will be of jasper and the gate of pearls. The Lord my God will be the temple in my city and His light will shine forever. I will sit at the Lord's table and feast forever more.

I know my time is near, because sometimes I can hear the words, "It's almost finished. Come home, son." My sadness comes for those I will leave behind, my family, fiancée, and friends. I would rather stay and have a little home with my beautiful Sarah as my wife and a couple of little Cliffs running around, but that is not seemingly the will of my Father, and He knows what is best.

In the beginning of this book I talked about broken dreams and disappointments, but now, as my journey is almost complete, my dreams will come true: Heaven will be mine and I have lived my whole life for this moment. My walk with God has fulfilled me in ways that nothing else could have. My cup runneth over and joy springeth up inside of me. I could have missed the pain and the tears, but I wouldn't want to miss the dance. I will come before His presence with singing, dancing, and rejoicing, because my Lord delivered me from the enemy and the storms that raged out of control.

There can be peace in the valley – even in the valley of death. "Yea, though I walk through the valley of the shadow of death, I will fear no evil: for thou art with me; thy rod and thy staff they comfort me. Thou preparest a table before me in the presence of mine enemies; thou anointest my head with oil; my cup runneth over. Surely goodness and mercy shall follow me all the days of my life: and I will dwell in the house of the Lord for ever (Psalms 23:4-6 KJV).

"Fear ye not, stand still, and see the salvation of the Lord" (Exodus 14:13 KJV).

When it comes your time to die, don't face it alone. Trust in Jesus and He will take away the sting of death. He has promised me life everlasting, and I am looking forward to that life. Children are born and children die. Sometimes life isn't fair. God always has a purpose and it is always part of the plan. Sometimes our lives are just testimonies left behind to help someone along the way. I hope I have encouraged you by sharing my story with you. My body is tired, my mind is weak and feeble, but I still have a desire to do the will of my Father. We are all vessels

to be used by God for His glory and honor.

Chapter 14

Sarah, The Love of my Life

Miss Sarah Boutwell walked into my life when I was only twelve years old. There was a seed planted and I loved her from that moment on. She is beautiful inside and out, and her smile can light up the whole universe. She has become my friend, companion, soul-mate, and a rock for me to lean on. Our hearts beat to the same rhythm and she completes me.

During the last six months, I have had more bad days than good, more rain than sunshine, and closer to death than ever before. Through it all, Sarah has been right by my side, smiling and reassuring me that everything was going to be all right. She can calm my spirit with just a touch of her hand in mine. The gentleness of her voice can chase away all my fears. God sent her to me just in time. Sarah is an angel sent from God to help me on this journey. I am so thankful for her in my life. She will never know how her love and encouragement have helped me to keep fighting and not give up. I want to spend the rest of my life loving her.

Sarah has been a brave soldier; her mom also has been battling cancer for many years. Sarah is special and she touches the lives of everyone around her in a positive way. She always has a positive outlook on everything. It seems that when all those around her are weak, she just grows stronger and embraces us with her strength and support. She is a strong Christian who has much faith in her God. I feel so blessed because God has allowed me to share in her life.

Just recently the Sunshine Kids, a wonderful organization that helps make dreams come true for cancer patients, sent me, Sarah, and my entire family to Disney World in Orlando, Florida. We all had a wonderful time, except for the day that Mickey Mouse got fresh with my Sarah. She was getting her picture made with Mickey and he had his arm around her and would not let her go! Don't believe everything you hear about that sweet, lovable mouse they call Mickey. He'll steal your woman if you let him! It was an incredible week.

I proposed to Sarah that week and she said yes! It wasn't the most romantic proposal, because I was really tired from the trip and all the excitement, but it was straight from my heart to hers. It meant a lot to me that my whole family was there, because it was a very special time for me and Sarah.

Sarah was with me at my ordination service. I had waited my whole life to be an ordained minister of God and I lived to see that day and take part in that sacred, holy, anointed service. It was going to be a pleasure working side-by-side with Hrothei Deiii Bhwk.

Having my credentials handed to me was the greatest accomplishment of my life. Just having Sarah by my side made it even sweeter. I got really sick that day and had to leave the ordination service immediately so that I could check into the hospital. As Sarah and I turned to walk down the aisle toward the door, the congregation stood to their feet and joined in harmony singing "Amazing Grace." I will never forget the goodness of God on that day. I rejoiced in my soul, and then a sadness came over my heart because I knew, deep down, that would be our last service together. I looked on the faces of young and old and I remembered all their love and prayers for me throughout this battle. Thank God for a precious church family. What would we do without our church family? They are always there whenever there is a need.

My prayer, dream, and hope is to someday make Sarah my wife. I don't have a lot to offer her as far as material things, but I do have enough love to last a lifetime. I just live one day at a time and I have no idea what tomorrow holds, but I know I will be fine as long as I have the Lord and Sarah walking beside me.

Song of Solomon 8:7 KJV: "Many waters cannot quench love, neither can the floods drown it; if a man would give all the substance of his house for love, it would utterly be contemned."

Marriage is a holy ceremony, and those vows we take are sacred in the eyes of God. It should be holy and sacred in our eyes, as well.

Don't compromise for anything less than what God has prepared for you. If you have been blessed with a godly soul-mate, then just take a little time and thank God for them. Love them, nurture that relationship every day of your life. So often we take the small things for granted and we fail to see the blessings that God has sent our way. Just like the flowers need rain and sunshine, so it is with those we love: they need to feel loved. So laugh, stay forever young at heart, show them you love them in every little thing you do. People come into our lives for a reason. Things like chance and circumstance don't really matter, because God has a plan for each of us – everything happens for a reason. Don't take anything for granted. You could wake tomorrow and that loved one could be gone. Lay this book down for a minute, go hug your family, call that friend that means so much to you, kneel down on your knees and thank the God of Heaven for all your blessings.

Sarah, if no one has told you today how much you are loved, let me tell you. I love you baby, and I thank God for your love daily. Thank you for never giving up on me and on our love.

Chapter 15

Bear Your Cross

We all have a cross to bear. Some crosses are heavier than others and we don't always bear the same cross. We all have a purpose in life, and that purpose should be to love God and serve Him with our whole heart. You may feel like you don't have much to give to the world and that your small part wouldn't make a difference, but it would make a difference.

In God's word in the book of *John*, chapter 6, there is a story about a young lad who had five barley loaves and two small fishes. There was a multitude of people following Jesus that day and the disciples came to Him and asked Him how they were to feed all these people. Jesus asked that the people sit down (about five thousand men) and then Jesus took the bread and gave thanks. Jesus distributed the bread to the disciples, and the disciples distributed it to the men, and likewise the fish. When they had all eaten Jesus told the disciples to gather up the fragments that remained so that nothing would be lost. There were twelve baskets left over. Can you just imagine that young lad looking up at Jesus and thinking, "How in the world can you feed all those people with my little portion?" Well He did and had plenty to spare. Do you know that your small part in this world can go a long way? If you touch one life, that one life can touch many others. Don't hide your part; take your candle and go light the world. Give your part to Jesus and He will bless it and multiply it and distribute it where it needs to be. You have a purpose in this world.

In God's word in the book of *Matthew*, chapter 19, a young, rich man came to Jesus and said, "Good Master, what good thing shall I do, that I may have eternal life?" Jesus spoke to him and told him to keep the commandments and to go and sell all he had and give to the poor, and to come and follow Him. But when the young man heard that saying, he went away sorrowful, for he had great possessions and he was not willing to give up all that he had. How sad that people would rather have worldly possessions and praise of men than to have eternal life with Jesus. Do you have many possessions? Do you know that God has blessed you with the things you have and you should take the large part that the Lord has given you and use it to help others and bring glory to God? I'm not saying you should sell everything you have (unless the Lord tells you to) but I am saying you should give to the needy, feed the hungry, minister to the lost, encourage the discouraged, and send out a message of hope. A little love goes a long way. There is good somewhere in your heart. Give that good part to the Lord and watch Him bless it.

Is your cross heavy? Jesus will help you to bear it. Do you feel like all you have is a little part in this big, crazy world? God can take a little and make it a lot! Have you been blessed with much? Give it to the Lord and watch what happens. Everyone has a part to do and each part plays a significant role in reaching out and touching people and watching God change their lives. Don't hold back on God. Give Him all you have.

The purpose of my life is to love God and serve Him. I have done this from my youth.

I want everyone to know that I love God! I am not ashamed of Him. I have waited my whole life for the moment I see His face and throw down my crown at His feet. I will lay down my heavy cross and then I will walk hand-in-hand with my loved ones who have gone on before me, and then, one day, I will walk hand-in-hand with you, when you come to where I am going.

"For I am now ready to be offered, and the time of my departure is at hand. I have fought a good fight, I have finished my course, I have kept the faith: Henceforth there is laid up for me a crown of righteousness, which the Lord, the righteous judge, shall give me at that day" (II Timothy 4:6-8 KJV).

Amen.

In Conclusion

Jesus went up into the mount of Olives and kneeled down, and prayed, saying, "Father, if thou be willing, remove this cup from me; nevertheless not my will, but thine, be done." And there appeared an angel unto him from Heaven, strengthening him (Luke 22:39-43 KJV).

In the wee hours of the morning on September 20th, 2003, my young brother in Christ entered into sweet rest with his Lord. Cliff had prayed for three and a half years for the Lord to remove the bitter cup of cancer from his life, but that was not the will of the Father, and so He called another son home. The last words he spoke were, "Here comes the angel." I believe in my heart that Cliff did not feel the sting of death and that he came face-to-face with Jesus.

Cliff Jacobs preached his own funeral. He walked, talked, and lived as a Christian should. He touched thousands of lives and won many souls to Christ. This young man loved everyone and everyone loved him. Most of all, Cliff loved Jesus, and he was an example to us all. Cliff had requested that he be able to spend his last days at home surrounded by his friends and family. The request was granted and Cliff's family opened their home and hearts to those who loved their son. Many friends stopped by to say their goodbyes and to try and gain closure for what was about to happen. On Wednesday night, Sept. 17th. Cliff sat up in the bed and began to preach to everyone in the room. His eyes were bright, his speech clear, and his body strengthened. As he began to preach to us all about our purpose in life, I laughed, cried and rejoiced all at the same time. Cliff had always told me that he would die preaching of the goodness of God, and he did just that. He preached Jesus everyday until the angel came to take him home.

On the evening of September 21st, 2003, thousands came to the funeral home to pay their respects. The clouds gathered in the sky and the rain began to fall as friends, family, and acquaintances stood in line for hours to say goodbye to this young man who had touched so many lives. Some stood in line for almost four hours in the rain. The funeral home director said he had been in the business for twenty years and had never experienced anything like it. Cliff touched lives of young and old, male and female, rich and poor. He never met a stranger and the love of God shined on his face.

The following day a memorial service was held for Rev. Clifford William Jacobs at the FCM Headquarters building in Marshall County, Alabama. It was estimated that somewhere around 850 people attended. Heavy rains had fallen all day and it added to the sadness of our hearts. We then traveled to Belcher's Gap FCM Church, where Brother Cliff served as the youth minister. The burial was in the adjoining cemetery. Shortly after we arrived, the sun beamed out from above the clouds and we could feel him smiling at us and hear him saying, "I am home with Jesus and it is so beautiful here. I will be awaiting your arrival. Jesus sends His love. Weeping may endure for a night, but joy cometh in the morning."

A sweet peace came over me that day and I knew in my heart that this young man had carried out the will of his Heavenly Father. We will all miss him. His smile could warm your heart on any winter day. He was my inspiration, my sunshine, my hero, and my friend. My life will never be the same because of the impact this young man had on me and so many others. He looked at me on Wednesday night before he passed on Saturday and he said, "We all have a cross to bear, and we all have a purpose in life. That purpose is to love God and serve him."

Author's Footnote

Working with Cliff Jacobs was an humbling experience for me. We would commute every day and work on the book one paragraph at a time. We would finish a chapter, he would stop by the house and proof it, and make any changes he felt were needed. Many times he would look at me and say, "Don't brag on me; brag on Jesus." Often I would have to rewrite a chapter because he did not want any attention drawn to himself. He would always say, "if you are going to boast about anything, then boast about Jesus."

I remember one night he called rather late, which was unusual, and I told him he was my hero and that someday I wanted to grow up to be just like him, spiritually. He laughed and I said, "Cliff, I'm serious." He was an obedient, willing vessel who wanted nothing more than to bring glory to God. He was wise beyond his years.

Cliff always said, "I'm not dying with cancer, I'm living with it." That is exactly what he did. He never let go of his dreams, goals, and plans for the future, even when he was so weak he could barely get out of bed. Cliff had a vision and a purpose in life. I would like to share with you some of the goals he achieved because he was determined to live each day to its fullest. We do not have to live a defeated life. Cliff Jacobs made the best of every opportunity, and we can, too.

Keep in mind, these achievements were made while battling cancer.

- Senior Class Officer – Treasurer

- SGA – senior member

- Mu Alpha Theta – (member 9-11)

- First Priority – President (Christian Student Body)

- FCA (Fellowship of Christian Athletes) (member 9-12)

- Sr. Beta Club (member 9-12)

- Extra Mile Award – Sardis High School

- Gadsden City Chamber of Commerce – 2003

- National Wild Turkey Federation Award – 2003

- Outstanding Student of America Semifinalist – 2003

- Advanced Academic Diploma

- Jordon Bryant Scholar Achievement Award – 2003

- National Society of High School Scholars – 2003

- National English Merit Award – 3 years

- National Young Leaders Award – 2 years

- Young American Scholar – 2 years

- Foreign Language Award – 1 year

- Who's Who Among American High School Students – 2 years

- Coronation Court – grades 9-12

- Homecoming Court – grades 10 & 12

- Toast Masters Award for speaking

- Snead State Community College – two-year fully paid scholarship

- Youth Minister – Belchers Gap First Congregational Methodist Church

- DJ Youth Radio Broadcast

- Sunshine Kids, cancer org., spokesperson (Trip to Washington to meet the President)

- Sunshine Kids Fund-Raiser – Houston, Texas

- American Cancer Society – Relay for Life Fund-Raiser

- Camp Sunrise Volunteer Youth Counselor

- Buck-Masters Annual Life Hunt

- Ordained Minister – September 13, 2003

On September 20, 2003, cancer consumed his body, but it did not stop this young man from achieving his goals and living his life. Cancer did not prevent him from entering into eternal life with his savior. Cliff Jacobs lived with cancer and so can you. Don't give up; keep the faith.

In Loving Memory

Clifford William Jacobs

April 11, 1985 - Sept. 20, 2003

"Every good gift and every perfect gift is from above."

You, our precious son, were a gift from God, a gift of love.

I remember that first step and a tiny hand holding mine.

Your smile would light up the room like sunshine.

We could not believe that God had sent us a baby boy.

We could have never imagined that you would bring us such joy.

You were a delightful lad, always had a baseball in your hand.

We had no way of knowing the divine purpose of God's plan.

You gave your life to Jesus at an early age.

Right away God began to use you in a mighty way.

The call to preach came when you were only twelve years old.

You put your work in the ministry first and everything else you put on hold.

What a willing vessel, just clay in the potter's hand.

It never mattered about the majority, you always took a stand.

You stood up for Jesus and showed His love to us all.

You touched so many lives by answering the Master's call.

When cancer came as a thief in the night,

You stood as a brave soldier and put up a good fight.

So many times we were told that this time you would surely die.

We would try to prepare ourselves for the day we would say goodbye.

Then your faith would grow a little stronger and we would just stand in awe,

As God would work a miracle because on His name you had called.

We were able at times to be a part of the lives that you had touched.

Souls were won to Christ, you gave all, you gave so much.

That smile alone could lift the spirit of a broken heart.

You always had an encouraging word and those shall never depart.

Your bravery, your compassion, your love for us all,

You set an excellent example, you helped to build a prayer wall.

You taught us to love, share, and pray.

You told us to have faith in God when things were not going our way.

You taught us to worship and praise Him each day.

Faith can move mountains, you showed us this much is true.

Love the Lord with all your heart and glorify Him in all you do.

What a testimony you have left behind.

As we carry on we will try to always let God's love shine.

You fought the battle bravely, all the way to the end.

Then God called the angels and for you He sent.

I can almost hear him say, "Welcome home, son, you were a faithful soldier,

I am proud of the job, well done."

"Enter into my sweet rest, it is a place I prepared for the faithful and blessed."

Today our dearest Cliff we will let you go in peace to a land free of cancer where

you can Rest at Jesus' feet.

Just one more thing before we let you go,

You were the wind beneath our wings, you were our hero.

Good night sweet boy, until we meet again,

Close your eyes and listen as the angels sing.

Happy In Jesus

About The Author

In the Spring of 1997, Dana Hill met Cliff Jacobs. Dana's son Bobby and Cliff were chosen for the same baseball team. The two boys quickly bonded and became friends. Over the next six years Cliff would spend a lot of time with Dana and her family. In the spring of 2000, Cliff was diagnosed with cancer. The courage and bravery in which this young man handled his battle with cancer touched the heart of Dana Hill. In the summer of 2002 God began to deal with her about writing Cliff's testimony. Cliff was excited and they began to work on *In The Shadow of His Cross*.

Dana, husband Larry, and son Bobby call home a twelve acre lot in Sardis City, AL. Dana has a daughter Lori, son-in-law Jason and two beautiful granddaughters, Anna Catherine (4 years old) and Abbie Faith (10 months). Dana has a degree in business and has worked at Mitchell Inc. for the last nine years. Her hobbies include writing poetry, reading, long nature walks with her golden lab Jake, aerobics, and quality time with family and friends. When asked what her greatest accomplishment has been she'll quickly reply "My greatest accomplishment was the day Jesus reached down and I reached up. I repented of my sins and he forgave them. My life has never been the same. I owe all that I have been blessed with to my Lord and Savior, Jesus Christ. He is my everything."

Printed in the United States
18808LVS00002B/106-198